to GREG

from Donna

Happy Anniversary!

2003

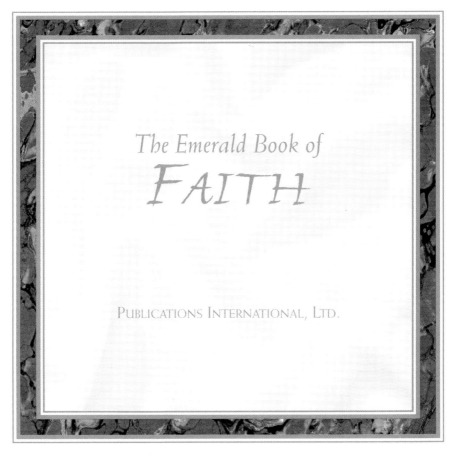

The Emerald Book of
FAITH

PUBLICATIONS INTERNATIONAL, LTD.

Photo credits: Front cover: **Michael Orton/Tony Stone Images** (center); **Sacco Productions Limited/Chicago** (background).

FPG International: Color Box; Michael Malyszko; Planet Earth Pictures; Richard Price; Telegraph Colour Library; VCG; **International Stock**: Wayne Aldridge; Scott Barrow; Mitch Diamond; Chad Ehlers; Andre Jenny; Mark Newman; Orion; Richard Pharaoh; Wood Sabold; Hardie Truesdale; **Herve Pelletier/SuperStock**.

Manufactured in China.

8 7 6 5 4 3 2 1

ISBN: 0-7853-3737-7

Original inspirations written by:

Elaine Creasman is a writer and poet. She writes for a variety of inspirational magazines including *Guideposts* and *Decision.*

Lain Chroust Ehmann is a columnist for the *San Jose Mercury News.* She writes on inspirational topics for numerous publications.

Margaret Anne Huffman is an award-winning writer and journalist. She has authored and contributed to numerous titles including *Simple Wisdom, Graces,* and *Family Celebrations.*

Marie Jones is a published writer of fiction and non-fiction stories as well as the author of several screenplays.

Other quotations compiled by Cathy Ann Tell.

*Faith requires personal commitment,
decision, and purpose. God sets the plan,
but we must do the legwork.*

When we believe in a power greater than ourselves, the entire universe moves to reveal the brilliant handiwork of a loving and creative master walking alongside us and guiding our way.

Faith is love taking the form of aspiration.

—WILLIAM ELLERY CHANNING

Faith is like the wind.
We hear its presence, see its power, feel its
effect on the world around us. We cannot
see it, but we know it is there.

*If there is a faith that can move mountains,
it is faith in your own power.*

—MARIE EBNER VON ESCHENBACH

Faith flows as I stop depending on what I think, on what I feel, on what I see and instead embrace these facts: God loves me. He will never leave me. He wants only the best for me.

Faith is neither proven through logic nor reason; it must be felt with the heart.

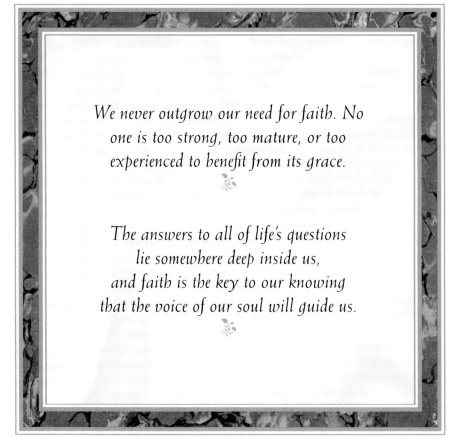

*We never outgrow our need for faith. No
one is too strong, too mature, or too
experienced to benefit from its grace.*

*The answers to all of life's questions
lie somewhere deep inside us,
and faith is the key to our knowing
that the voice of our soul will guide us.*

*Blessed are those who have not seen and
yet have come to believe.*

—JOHN 20:29

*Faith empowers me
to leap across
the chasms in my life
and to have the confidence
that I'll make it to the other side
—and to believe that
the other side exists.*

*The eyes of faith
see things
not as they are,
but as they could be.*

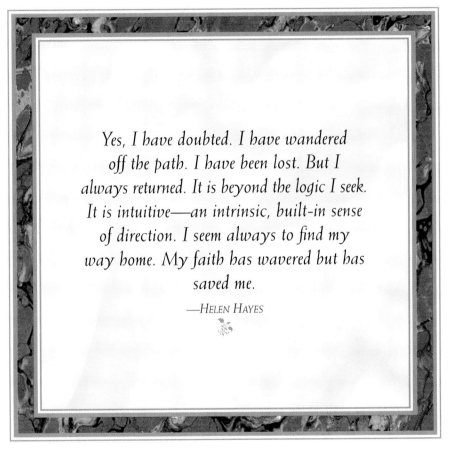

*Yes, I have doubted. I have wandered
off the path. I have been lost. But I
always returned. It is beyond the logic I seek.
It is intuitive—an intrinsic, built-in sense
of direction. I seem always to find my
way home. My faith has wavered but has
saved me.*

—HELEN HAYES

From each of life's misfortunes,
large or small, comes a new beginning,
an opportunity to renew your
faith in the future.

When the world around us grows cold and
chaotic, faith is the balm that soothes a
fearful heart and the blanket that comforts
an anxious mind.

Great faith is not found; it is made of
tiny demonstrations of commitment on a
daily basis.

. . . whenever you face trials of any kind,
consider it nothing but joy, because you
know that the testing of your faith
produces endurance; and let endurance
have its full effect, so that you may be
mature and complete, lacking in nothing.

—JAMES 1:2–4

Faith is the force of life.

—LEO TOLSTOY

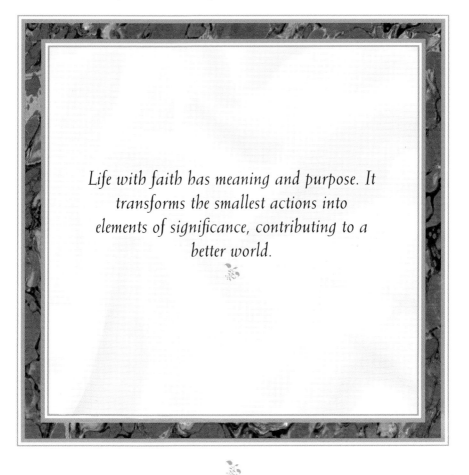

Life with faith has meaning and purpose. It transforms the smallest actions into elements of significance, contributing to a better world.

One miracle is just as easy to believe as
another.

—WILLIAM JENNINGS BRYAN

*Faith in God's love
frees me to be the real me,
for I remember that God sees me as I am
and loves me with all His heart.*

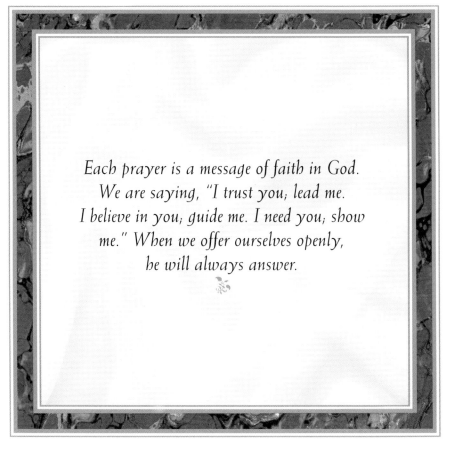

Each prayer is a message of faith in God.
We are saying, "I trust you; lead me.
I believe in you; guide me. I need you; show
me." When we offer ourselves openly,
he will always answer.

The principal part of faith is patience.

—GEORGE MACDONALD

Where there is lack,
Faith shouts "Abundance!"
Where there is despair,
Faith sings out "Joy!"
Where there is fear,
Faith whispers "Courage."
Where there is animosity,
Faith affirms only LOVE.

Faith is like a tiny seed of belief inside us that grows into a mighty tree, each leaf a new direction, each branch a new opportunity.

Every soul is a melody which needs renewing.

—STÉPHANE MALLARMÉ

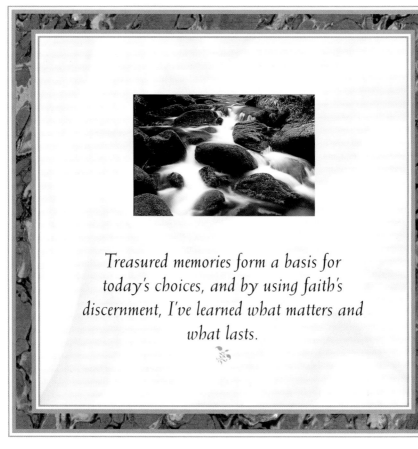

Treasured memories form a basis for
today's choices, and by using faith's
discernment, I've learned what matters and
what lasts.

*Now faith is the assurance of things hoped
for, the conviction of things not seen.*

—*HEBREWS 11:1*

Like the lighthouse beacon, faith guides our way through the fog of fear, doubt, and uncertainty to the sea of clarity beyond.

Faith perceives a truth that lies beyond our field of vision—a truth only our heart has eyes to see.

When the doors of perception have opened
and the windows of faith have been
cleansed,
we will know that our souls are eternal
and that our life never ends.

Just a tiny seed of faith, watered with love,
wisdom, and hard work, grows into a
majestic tree of blessings.

The words which express our faith and
piety are not definite; yet they are
significant and fragrant like frankincense
to superior natures.

—HENRY DAVID THOREAU

Faith does not fear change, but knows that
all change is simply the spirit's way
of moving our life in the direction of
our destiny.

*Faith makes the discords of the present
the harmonies of the future.*

—ROBERT COLLYER

Faith is a silent declaration of inner wholeness amidst the outer appearance of chaos and disorder.

Faith is the highest passion in a human being. Many in every generation may not come that far, but none comes further.

—SØREN KIERKEGAARD

*Faith is leaning on the only one who
is able to hold me up.*

Faith can give us courage to face the uncertainties of the future.

—MARTIN LUTHER KING, JR.

Faith has moved mountains, healed hearts
And saved men from the sword.
With this power we need not search
For answers outside of the Lord.

A wise mind knows that adverse events are blessed opportunities for growth in disguise.

Real faith is not only words spoken but an inner confidence embraced and cherished by the heart.

One needs to feel that one's life has
meaning, that one is needed in this world.

—HANNAH SENESH

Faith is my soul's good friend that urges
me on, convincing me I will victoriously
reach the finish line in this race called
my life.

And without faith it is impossible to please God, for whoever would approach him must believe that he exists and that he rewards those who seek him.

—HEBREWS 11:6

*Faith grows as I do the simple things
I know how to do.*

Faith delivers us from sad yesterdays and sends us toward happy tomorrows.

Unseen, yet felt on the face like a summer breeze, faith lifts and supports, filling spirits with assurance.

Faith is a true sign of bravery. It is looking forward to the future despite challenges and adversity; it is trusting in something that you can neither see nor touch yet knowing it is always there guiding you along life's path.

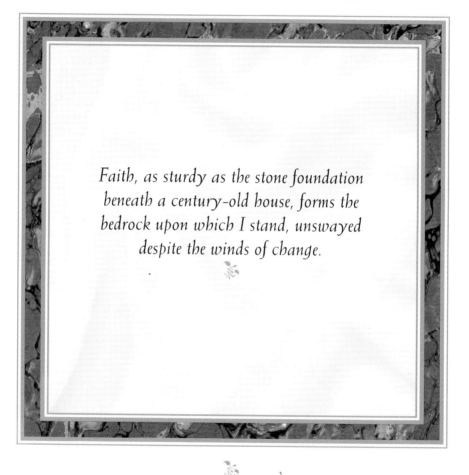

Faith, as sturdy as the stone foundation beneath a century-old house, forms the bedrock upon which I stand, unswayed despite the winds of change.